Lessons My Toddler Taught Me

Lessons My Toddler Taught Me

A Devotional for **Mothers** of Young Children

Anita S. Lane

A Division of WINEPRESS PUBLISHING

Pleasant Word (a division of WinePress Publishing, PO Box 428, Enumclaw, WA 98022) functions only as book publisher. As such, the ultimate design, content, editorial accuracy, and views expressed or implied in this work are those of the author.

ISBN 13: 978-1-4141-0927-5
ISBN 10: 1-4141-0927-X
Library of Congress Catalog Card Number: 2006910970

8·26·09

Gail,

Life is full of Lessons. Enjoy!

LB

Anita S Lane

Turning the challenge of rearing toddlers
into a time of spiritual growth!

PO · JC.8

Dedication

To my children who teach me so much each day—Ania, Terrence II, Daniel and Joshua—and to my husband, Terrence, who is all that I dreamed of in a husband and father.

Table of Contents

Acknowledgements

Paulette A. Foster—Mom, life's most important lessons I learned from you. Thank you for being an awesome woman. I'm still striving to be like you. Thank you, also, for editing this manuscript every step of the way. Your steadfast encouragement and support have helped keep my dream alive.

Virginia Fabin—with four young children at home it's often difficult to accomplish the *essentials*, let alone write a book. Thus, I am very grateful for your dedicated care of my children while I labored at the library to complete the manuscript. I couldn't have done it without you.

Introduction

Lessons *My Toddler Taught Me* is about making sense of the wondrous and challenging season of toddlerhood. As the stay-at-home mother of four young children I find myself constantly responding to and answering a barrage of comments and questions from wide-eyed toddlers with boundless energy.

This season of life can be mentally, emotionally and physically exhausting. Yet, so often out of our children's mouths come the cutest little phrases. Those phrases have become the foundation for this devotional.

As parents, our number one priority is to meet the needs of our children and to cultivate bright, loving, respectful and generous contributors to our society. Yet, our energy is so focused on raising great children that we sometimes forget, in order to successfully fulfill this priority, we must first be *great* ourselves. Thus, this devotional aims to help us dedicate a few minutes each day towards becoming that *great* woman and mom our children can emulate.

May this season of fascinating growth for your toddler also be a season of fascinating, spiritual growth for you.

Anita S. Lane

How to use this devotional

It is my prayer that this devotional will serve as a 60-day mommy boost—a tool that God can use to facilitate spiritual growth.

A Daily Action Step

After each devotional is a page for you to write down one thing you will do *today* in response to what you have read. While you may have been challenged to make a change in more than one area, choose just one area upon which you will focus and work towards improving *today*.

At the bottom of the page is space for you to record an answered prayer or progress you've made in that area. You can revisit and complete this section days, weeks or months later—whenever you witness results.

During these sixty days I pray that you'll seize each learning opportunity with your child as a learning opportunity for yourself. Our daily parenting challenges can stump us or spur us to spiritual growth. So let's grow!

"Mommy, I don't like it..."

I had just purchased two of those pricey, fresh fruit smoothies at the mall. I just knew my children would enjoy this special treat. After all, I shelled out six bucks to get both of them one. Instead, they both said, "Mommy, I don't like it. Can I have water?" Boy, did I feel silly. I went back to the counter and got each of them a courtesy cup of ice water.

I'm reminded of Luke 10:41-42, where Martha was busy making sure everything was just right and her sister Mary was sitting at Jesus' feet. Jesus told Martha, "One thing is needful, and Mary has chosen that good part."

If you are thirsty, water is all that is needed. In this instance, my children chose water. Children are simple. We complicate things. We are the ones that offer a plethora of styles, flavors and sizes in everything from food to clothes.

Likewise, there are a lot of things that we adults can get into in an effort to quench our thirst in life—careers, hobbies, relationships, church activities and the like. Yet Jesus reminds us that one thing is needful—to sit at His feet. Commune with Him. Learn from Him. When we seek God first and His righteousness, all of the other things we seek—fulfilled careers, relationships, health, wealth, etc.—are added to us. They are attracted to us. We draw them like a magnet. While the pricey things in life are nice, they are meaningless without the daily dose of water we need to exist.

> *"But whoever drinks of the water that I shall give him will never thirst. But the water that I shall give him will become in him a fountain of water springing up into everlasting life."*
>
> (John 4:14 NKJV)

Prayer: Lord, I quiet my spirit before you. I humble myself and let go of the cares of this world to sit at your feet and learn from you. Though things may be hurried around me, inwardly I will remain still and open to your voice.

Lesson Application

Date: _____

Today I will:

_____

_____

_____

_____

_____

_____

_____

Progress Made/Prayer Answered:

Date: _____

_____

_____

_____

_____

_____

_____

"Daddy, don't sit on Sweetheart!"

Daddy, don't sit on Sweetheart!" my two-year-old daughter warned as her father opened the van door and proceeded to sit in the driver's seat.

Daddy promptly picked up Sweetheart and gently handed her to his anxious toddler. The intriguing part to this story is that Daddy could not see Sweetheart. Sweetheart was our daughter's imaginary playmate. Nevertheless, Daddy responded to his daughter's request. He promptly obeyed although he did not see.

How often does God give us a gentle warning in our spirit, "Don't do this. Do this. Go another direction." Yet many times we do not obey because we do not see what God sees. From our perspective all is well. There is nothing about which to be concerned. Yet, this is why God is God and we are not. He can see the future and knows how to direct us to His intended destination for us. All we have to do is trust and obey.

> *"Trust in the LORD with all your heart, and lean not on your own understanding; In all your ways acknowledge Him, and He shall direct your paths."*
> (Proverbs 3:5-6 NKJV)

Prayer: Lord, I commit this day to you. Steer me towards your will for me and away from anything that is wrong for me. I will trust and obey—even if I do not see.

Lesson Application

Date: _____

Today I will:

_____

_____

_____

_____

_____

_____

_____

Progress Made/Prayer Answered:

Date: _____

_____

_____

_____

_____

_____

_____

"Thank you."

My infant daughter's first recognizable words outside of *Dada* and *Mama* were, "Thank you." Of course the consonants and vowels were not fully enunciated, but it was clear to almost everyone what she was saying. And she would say it all the time. She would say it when you gave her something and even when you took something away.

As Christians, the phrase *thank you* is one of the first things we say to God. At the point of becoming a Christian we begin to recognize just how much God loves us. We're grateful for our new lives in Christ. We're grateful for our new family in Christ. We're grateful for another chance. We're grateful for another day to serve Him. Our immense sense of gratitude is apparent for all to see. We've been redeemed and we're so glad about it!

The key is to maintain that attitude of gratitude as we mature as Christians. Just as my infant who said, "Thank you," whether something was given to her or taken away, we must learn to recognize God as sovereign and thank Him when things are going well and continue to thank Him when times are difficult. Every day we must determine to remind ourselves of the things for which we are to be grateful and focus on those things.

It could be worse—even if it doesn't seem like it. Our grateful attitude in the midst of trial or tribulation demonstrates to God that we trust Him and have faith in His role as a loving Father. When times are hard we must also learn to thank God for the lessons we will learn and the growth we'll experience from that time of trial. Our continual "thank you" releases a positive response from God and good things inevitably follow.

> *"In all things give thanks. For this is the will of God in Christ Jesus concerning us."*
> (1 Thessalonians 5:18 KJV)

Prayer: Lord, thank you for this day you have given me. I thank you that whether or not I like everything that comes my way I will grow and become a better person as a result. I thank you that you know what is best for me and you have my best interest at heart.

Lesson Application

Date: _____

Today I will:

_____

_____

_____

_____

_____

_____

_____

Progress Made/Prayer Answered:

Date: _____

_____

_____

_____

_____

_____

_____

"I can't do it!"

When my first child was learning to put on her socks she often had a difficult time—especially trying to get the sock line on the top of her toes. It would frustrate her to no end. She would try and try to make it work and complain all the while.

"Mommy I can't do it."

"Do you want me to help you?" I would ask.

"No," she would answer. Then she would try it again.

After a few minutes of this I would get frustrated myself.

"If you don't want me to help you why do you keep complaining to me?" I would say. I didn't quite understand it.

Then I thought about it. "Is this how God feels about us?" So often we make decisions to do things in life—often without consulting God first—and we're confronted with the consequences of those decisions. At other times we are just confronted with the unavoidable challenges of life. Then we try and try to make things work and they just do not seem to be working out. We keep having trouble and running into stumbling blocks. And what do we do? We complain.

"God, this isn't working," we say.

"Uh…this is so frustrating," we groan.

"I can't put up with this anymore," we pout.

God hears it all. Yet He's helpless to do anything about it because we have not invited Him to assist us. So He just stands by listening as we complain and wishing we would just ask Him for His guidance and help.

God created us as individuals with a free will. We are not His puppets—just like it is obvious our children will never be our puppets. We must make a decision to invite Him in for His guidance and help. He's so much better equipped to handle the circumstances we face just as we're so much better equipped to deal with our circumstances once we have solicited His assistance.

"Come to me, all you who labor and are heavy-laden and overburdened and I will cause you to rest. [I will ease and relieve and refresh your souls.] Take My yoke upon you and learn of Me, for I am gentle (meek) and humble (lowly) in heart, and you will find rest (relief and ease and refreshment and recreation and blessed quiet) for your souls. For My

11

yoke is wholesome (useful, good—not harsh, hard, sharp, or pressing, but comfortable, gracious and pleasant), and My burden is light and easy to be borne."

(Matthew 11:28-30 AMP)

Prayer: Lord, today I invite you in to help me with life's challenges. I acknowledge that I need your help to consistently do the right thing at the right time. I will rest knowing that with your help I will come through every situation I am facing. Thank you for helping me overcome each of today's obstacles, large or small.

Lesson Application

Date: _____

Today I will:

_____

_____

_____

_____

_____

_____

Progress Made/Prayer Answered:

Date: _____

_____

_____

_____

_____

_____

_____

"I went to the potty already."

More often than not this was the response my three-and-a-half-year-old would give when it was time to go to bed. Yes, she had gone to the potty, but it was more than an hour and a few drinks earlier. To her, however, it was good enough that she had gone, and she did not see the necessity of going again.

Sometimes we respond similarly to God when it seems that more effort is being required of us.

But God, I have done that already. I have prayed. I have had faith, we say. But being a disciple of Christ is not a one time event. Being a Christian is a relationship. What we do when we commence our relationship with Christ is what we must do—and even the more—to continue in our relationship with Him.

Jesus said in Matthew 8:31 that "If you continue in My word, then you are My disciples indeed..." The Word tells us that we must continue in faith (Colossians 1:23), continue in brotherly love (Hebrews 13:1), and continue in prayer (Romans 12:12). Ultimately, this is how we get God's results for our lives.

> *"And let us not be weary in well doing: for in due season we shall reap, if we faint not."*
>   (Galatians 6:9 KJV)

Prayer: Lord, forgive me for thinking that what I've done in the past is good enough for today. Help me to be faithful to do the things you require of me today. And help me to keep doing them over and over again until I achieve your desired result.

Lesson Application

Date: _____

Today I will:

_____

_____

_____

_____

_____

_____

_____

Progress Made/Prayer Answered:

Date: _____

_____

_____

_____

_____

_____

_____

"I thought it was broken!"

As my husband was leaving for work one morning, we found ourselves scouring the house for his mobile phone. Finally, I asked my three year old if she had seen it. As she began walking towards the tall white trash can, she said, "Mommy, it is right here."

I began to search the trash and to my surprise I uncovered the mobile phone.

"Why did you put Daddy's phone in the trash?" I asked.

"It didn't work," she said. "I thought it was broken."

I picked it up and turned it on. "It works just fine," I said.

My husband and I were utterly amazed that our daughter would actually put his phone in the trash.

Didn't she know better than that? But then again, when she pushed the buttons nothing happened. So from her viewpoint it didn't work and when things stop working, Mommy and Daddy usually throw them away.

As humans, we are often quick to discount and discard something in our lives because it is "not working" or we don't like the way it is working. It may be a relationship, a new business venture or a parenting strategy. We must remember to constantly consult our owner and the owner's manual for insight and instructions. God holds the key to making things work out for our good. He grants us the grace to endure the seasons when things do not appear to be working.

> *"If any of you lack wisdom, let him ask of God, that giveth to all men liberally, and upbraideth not; and it shall be given him."*
>
> (James 1:5 KJV)

Prayer: Everything in my life that doesn't seem to be "working" I submit to you. I ask you for wisdom to deal appropriately with every relationship and situation. I thank you that all things will work together for my good in the end.

Lesson Application

Date: _____

Today I will:

_____

_____

_____

_____

_____

_____

_____

Progress Made/Prayer Answered:

Date: _____

_____

_____

_____

_____

_____

_____

"I want you to carry me, Daddy."

My daughter would often ask her father to carry her up the stairs at night when she was sleepy, tired, or afraid of the scary monsters. Being the proud papa he is, he would oblige and carry her to her place of rest.

There may be times in your life when you feel as though you need your heavenly Father to carry you. You may be facing the loss of a loved one, a serious illness or some other tumultuous circumstance and your own legs are just too feeble to carry you through. God is our proud Father. He is more than happy to carry us when we are weak. But it takes more than crying out; it takes cooperation. Just like my husband needs my daughter to wrap her legs around his waist, place her arms around his neck, and lean on him, God needs us to do the same.

"Draw close to me. Lean on me. Don't let go," God urges.

When we do this, God is able to help us fight our battles and overcome any situation. Stay in His word and draw strength from Him. Before you know it, you will arrive at a place of rest that you had not achieved before. You may think to yourself, "I'm not sure how I got here," when all the while God was carrying you through.

"And He said unto me, 'My grace is sufficient for thee: for My strength is made perfect in weakness.' Most gladly therefore will I rather glory in my infirmities, that the power of Christ may rest upon me."

(2 Corinthians 12:9 KJV)

Prayer: Lord, I thank you for carrying me through this situation. Alone, I am weak and I am weary. But, by your grace I am strong and I am empowered to face any circumstance.

Lesson Application

Date: _____

Today I will:

_____

_____

_____

_____

_____

_____

_____

Progress Made/Prayer Answered:

Date: _____

_____

_____

_____

_____

_____

_____

"Let me do it!"

When my first son was two years old, he enjoyed pushing the shopping cart at the store. The only problem was that he was not tall enough to see above the cart. If I did not put my hand on the cart to direct it, he would hit cars, adults, children, shelves and anything else in his path. But that did not matter to him. Whenever I attempted to help guide the cart, he would yell, "Let me do it!"

Without the guiding force of the Holy Spirit we make bad judgments. We are misguided and not only do we hurt ourselves, but we inadvertently hurt others as well. At times in our walk with God we are tempted to just "hang loose" and do our own thing. We want to do what we want, say what we feel, and live life according to our own standards. The problem is that we do not see the big picture.

God sees the future and wants to protect us from tomorrow's painful consequences, and the regrets that follow for actions taken and words spoken today. As Christians, we cannot live merely for ourselves. We must always be mindful of how our actions affect other people.

> *"He who heeds instruction and correction is [not only himself] in the way of life [but also] is a way of life for others. And he who neglects or refuses reproof [not only himself] goes astray [but also] causes to err and is a path toward ruin for others."*

(Proverbs 10:17 AMP)

Prayer: Dear Lord, as I go throughout this day, please be my guiding force. I submit my thoughts, my words and my actions to your will. Help me to heed instruction so that I can be an example that others can follow.

Lesson Application

Date: _____

Today I will:

_____

_____

_____

_____

_____

_____

_____

Progress Made/Prayer Answered:

Date: _____

_____

_____

_____

_____

_____

_____

"Mommy, my brother bit my toe! Now I'll have to hop around on one foot."

My three-year-old hopped into my room yelling that her two-year-old brother had bitten her toe. She was crying and moaning. I was beginning to get concerned. I wondered how badly she might have been bitten. Within a moment she and her brother wandered back into her room and I no longer heard her wails.

Then I heard her say, "Mommy, my brother said I'm sorry…" They immediately went back to playing and I never heard anything else about her bitten toe.

I was stunned. She had been hurt. She was in pain. Did all of the pain suddenly disappear? What happened? What I concluded was that most of her pain was psychological. The pain existed because her feelings had been hurt and she was offended.

"Mommy, my brother bit my toe! Now I'll have to hop around on one foot."

Once her brother apologized, she released it; the pain subsided and they resumed playing.

Too often we hold on to offenses and hurts, continuing to hop on one foot instead of letting go of those offenses and resuming a normal, healthy, pain-free life. Even if the person who offended us does not apologize, we must make a decision to forgive him or her, let it go and get back to living a full, abundant life.

> *"And when you stand praying, forgive, if ye have ought against any: that your father also which is in heaven may forgive you your trespasses."*
> (Mark 11:25 KJV)

Prayer: Today I make a decision to forgive those who have hurt and offended me. Whether or not they apologize, I will forgive, let go and not let the past hinder my glorious future. With your help Lord, I know it can be done.

Lesson Application

Date: _____

Today I will:

_____

_____

_____

_____

_____

_____

_____

Progress Made/Prayer Answered:

Date: _____

_____

_____

_____

_____

_____

_____

"I want somebody to play with me in my room."

Just before sunrise, one by one our children would migrate into our bedroom and climb up in Mommy and Daddy's big bed for their last bit of shut-eye. My daughter is typically the first to wake up and is eager to engage the rest of us in conversation and play. Since the rest of us aren't ready to get up yet, I encourage her to go to her room and play. Inevitably her response is, "But I want somebody to play with me in my room." I try to explain to her that if she wants to play when no one else is ready to, then she must play alone. It's OK to play alone.

There are times in our lives when we have an idea, an unction, a desire to step out and do something that may be a little different or more forward thinking than those around us. Instinctively we say to them, "Come on. Get up. Let's try this idea."

Others may not see what you see or may simply not be ready to get up yet. This is when your loyalty and character are tested. Will you be true to the One whom you believe blessed you with the idea? Will you have the fortitude and courage to step out and do what you believe you're called to do even if no one else sees it, understands it or wants to come with you? Remember, pioneers are called pioneers because they go first where others have not gone. There are times in your life when you have to step out on your own. You may feel lonely. But remember, you are never alone.

> *"Have I not commanded thee? Be strong and of a good courage; be not afraid, neither be thou dismayed: for the Lord thy God is with thee whithersoever thou goest."*
>
> (Joshua 1:9 KJV)

Prayer: Lord, help me to obey you even if it means stepping out on my own and going it alone. I know that you are with me and you will never leave nor forsake me.

Lesson Application

Date: _____

Today I will:

_____

_____

_____

_____

_____

_____

_____

Progress Made/Prayer Answered:

Date: _____

_____

_____

_____

_____

_____

_____

"Mommy, why are we going backwards?"

Often while riding in my parents' boat we would sit with the children at the rear of the boat and watch the large, white-capped waves created by the boat's movement. The boat was moving forward, but we were facing backwards. One day, my daughter looked up at me and asked, "Mommy, why are we going backwards?"

From the captain's perspective, at the helm, high above the rest of us, it is very clear that we are going forward and moving closer and closer to our destination. Those of us in the boat have put our lives in his hands and he's got it all under control. Nevertheless, to my little three-year-old, it appears as though we're going backwards.

Sometimes in our walk with God, we have put our lives in His hands and we know He is in control, yet it may appear as though we are going backwards. We take one step forward and two steps backward it seems. We feel there is always something hindering us from getting to our destination in the amount of time we would like to get there. But we must remember that God sits at the helm and can see our destination clearly before Him. The waves may come and we may get wet, but it is all part of the journey. Don't be tempted to take matters into your own hands. Remember, you *are* facing backwards. If you move forward, you will be headed in the wrong direction.

> *"For thou art my rock and my fortress; therefore for thy name's sake lead me, and guide me."*
> (Psalm 31:3 KJV)

Prayer: Heavenly Father, this day I place my life in your hands. I trust you are taking me closer and closer to my destination. I surrender the helm. Have thine own way.

Lesson Application

Date: _____

Today I will:

_____

_____

_____

_____

_____

_____

_____

Progress Made/Prayer Answered:

Date: _____

_____

_____

_____

_____

_____

_____

"I'm going to be on TV."

On week days my children would watch the morning line-up of Public Broadcasting Station's educational programming for children. My daughter always seemed to be fascinated by television and would always want to "get in" the television to play with the characters.

"Mommy, how do I get in there?" she would say. Eventually, one day she graduated to saying, "Mom, I'm going to be on TV."

"Really?" I said.

"Yes."

"What are you going to do on TV?" I asked.

To my surprise she answered, "I'm going to be the news." (She didn't say she would be on the news). I inferred from that statement she meant she would be one of the persons presenting the news.

To that I simply said, "OK."

Granted, my daughter was only three, but who could say at that point what she would actually grow up to be and do. It reminded me of the need for us to speak our futures into existence. If God has put something in your heart, He expects you to believe it, prepare for it, and speak it. Faith comes by hearing. And when you hear yourself say what you expect to become it is like adding fuel to the fire within you. Not only that, our faith gives God the ammunition He needs to fully perform what He has planned for our lives.

Just as with Abraham and Sarah, when God gave Abram a vision, they obeyed, changed their names, and began calling themselves the father and mother of many nations. And it happened just as God said.

> *"We having the same spirit of faith, according as it is written, I believed, and therefore have I spoken; we also believe, and therefore speak..."*
> (2 Corinthians 4:13 KJV)

Prayer: Lord I thank you for the visions and dreams you've placed in my heart. I believe, I will confess, and I will prepare. Show me this day what steps to take.

Lesson Application

Date: _____

Today I will:

_____

_____

_____

_____

_____

_____

Progress Made/Prayer Answered:

Date: _____

_____

_____

_____

_____

_____

_____

"OK, I'll do it right now!"

After repeatedly asking my three-year-old to do something—like put on her clothes or put away her toys—she would sense the urgency in my voice.

"OK, Mommy, I'll do it right now!" she'd say firmly.

I would think to myself, *Great, she's finally getting it.*

However, before long I would check back to see how she was progressing. Many times she would be watching television or playing with one of the toys she was supposed to be putting away. Seconds turned to minutes and minutes would turn to hours if I didn't intervene. It was very easy for her to get distracted.

God gives us assignments, too. The Word of God explicitly reveals God's will for us and as we read it we will find assignments for our daily lives—love, pray, obey, forgive, etc. We may hear an inspiring message over the pulpit and think, "OK, Lord, I'm going to do it. I'm going to start today!"

However, often we're not out of the church parking lot before we've met our first temptation and become distracted from the assignment God gave us.

Distractions come as a tool to get us off course and keep us out of God's perfect will for our lives. We must learn to discipline ourselves to stay on course and not be sidetracked no matter what comes our way or what other people may say or do.

> *"Let thine eyes look right on, and let thine eyelids look straight before thee...Turn not to the right hand nor to the left..."*
>
> (Proverbs 4:25, 27 KJV)

Prayer: Dear Lord, this day I seek your explicit will for my life. Help me to stay on course and not become distracted by the demands of life.

Lesson Application

Date: _____

Today I will:

_____

_____

_____

_____

_____

_____

_____

Progress Made/Prayer Answered:

Date: _____

_____

_____

_____

_____

_____

_____

"I want one!"

Almost daily my three-year-old would come to her Daddy and ask for money out of his pocket. It was a special treat for her. Soon her two-year-old brother realized he was missing out. One day he witnessed this transaction and immediately came over and wanted his.

"I want one!" he exclaimed. I guess he figured, *He is father to both of us, so if she gets one then I should get one too.*

Ultimately, his sister received three dollars, but he only got one. Why? She was more responsible with money.

It's the same way with God. Every child of God is not entitled to the same thing in the same proportion at the same time. There are contributing factors to the apparent blessings we receive in life—such as how responsible we are with what we already have, the law of sowing and reaping and even whether or not we have asked. Just like my children's natural father, God does not want to deny His children of anything as long as it fits into His purpose for their lives and they are responsible enough to handle it and do the right thing with it.

So the next time you see a fellow child of God get blessed and your immediate response is, "I want one!" ask yourself, "Am I ready? Have I proven myself responsible enough for this yet? Is this in line with God's purpose and plan for me?"

> *"And unto one he gave five talents, to another two, and to another one; to every man according to his several ability..."*
>
> (Matthew 25:15 KJV)

Prayer: Dear Lord, today I make the decision to be a good steward and to be fully responsible for all that you have given me. I know that what you have for me is for me, and everything I need for this life's journey will come in the appropriate time.

Lesson Application

Date: _____

Today I will:

_____

_____

_____

_____

_____

_____

Progress Made/Prayer Answered:

Date: _____

_____

_____

_____

_____

_____

_____

"Mommy...Mommy... Mommy...Mommy..."

There were days when my toddlers would seem to bombard me with an endless barrage of, "Mommy I don't want to ...Mommy, help me...Mommy, my brother...Mommy, my sister...Mommy, Mommy, Mommy!"

That was the relentless melody that rang all day long. Many times, I just gave up, conceded to defeat and sulked. *This is my fate—tomorrow will be better,* I'd think to myself.

However, that attitude didn't make matters any better. I eventually learned that on days like those, when the pressure seemed to mount, I could learn a thing or two from my children. So I began to call, "Father, Father, Father!" "Father, grant me grace...Father, grant me peace...Father, help me to walk in patience and love!"

Just as we hear our children and respond to their never-ending requests, our heavenly Father also will hear and respond if we seek Him. Oh, to be a child who doesn't fear crying out and asking for help time and time again, all day long. After all, that is the responsibility of loving parents—to be there when a child needs them. Likewise, our heavenly Father promises to hear us when we cry out to Him and be our help in our time of need…all day long.

"Trust in him at all times; ye people, pour out your heart before him: God is a refuge for us. Selah."
(Psalm 62:8 KJV)

Prayer: Dear heavenly Father, all the day long will I come to you and pour out my heart to you. I thank you that you always hear me and that I can find strength, peace and refuge in you.

Lesson Application

Date: _____

Today I will:

_____

_____

_____

_____

_____

_____

_____

Progress Made/Prayer Answered:

Date: _____

_____

_____

_____

_____

_____

_____

"I don't want to be a good girl anymore."

That's a good girl!" I said to my daughter in response to her sharing the last of the juice with her brother in the car.

"I don't want to be a good girl anymore!" she quickly responded.

How could she say that? I thought.

But she simply didn't want to share. If sharing juice with her brother meant being a good girl, she didn't want to be a good girl anymore. However, Mommy insisted.

As we traveled along, they continued to take turns sipping out of the cup. Before long, I noticed from my rearview mirror that my daughter was smiling. They had turned the requirement into a friendly game of *take a sip and hand it off*. Needless to say, both were no longer thirsty, and Mommy was pleased.

There may be times in our lives where we, too, must do what is required of us out of sheer obedience, even though it goes against the very fibers of our natural being. Obedience doesn't always feel good—it was very painful for my daughter at first. But each time we obey, it gets easier and easier. Once we establish a habit of hearing and obeying God, it can become a joy in and of itself. Obedience can become a delight.

> *"Though he were a Son, yet learned he obedience by the things which he suffered."*
> (Hebrews 5:8 KJV)

Prayer: Lord, this day help me to obey you instantly, wholly and joyfully— that I might learn genuine obedience and benefit from its rewards.

Lesson Application

Date: _____

Today I will:

_____

_____

_____

_____

_____

_____

_____

Progress Made/Prayer Answered:

Date: _____

_____

_____

_____

_____

_____

_____

"I need help doing it..."

Beginning at age two, my daughter had the responsibility of making up her bed. By age three, she was an old pro at it. However, one morning when I recited the words, "Make up your bed," within a few seconds she came to me and said, "I need help doing it."

I was struck by the fact that she didn't spend a lot of time laboring at the task. She didn't get frustrated. She wasn't whining. She came directly to me in a matter-of-fact tone and said she needed help. I said, "OK" and the mission was accomplished without much travail. As it turned out, her flat sheet and comforter were no longer tucked under at the end of the bed. She couldn't simply pull them up as she usually did.

How great would it be to always enlist God's help at the onset of a task—at the very beginning before we've exerted much energy or time, or made a mess of things. It should be very obvious to us when we're dealing with something out of our league. And, if we're honest, even the things we think we can handle are still best handled with grace and wisdom of God.

Instead of taking on the "He-Man" or "She-Man" role, become as a child and simply ask and receive God's help. It will make the task much easier.

"For the Lord God will help me; therefore shall I not be confounded: therefore have I set my face like a flint, and I know that I shall not be ashamed."
(Isaiah 50:7 KJV)

Prayer: Dear Lord, I know that you are present this day to help me with my every task. I enlist your help. Thank you for providing the wisdom, understanding and guidance I need.

Lesson Application

Date: _____

Today I will:

_____

_____

_____

_____

_____

_____

_____

Progress Made/Prayer Answered:

Date: _____

_____

_____

_____

_____

_____

_____

"But Mommy..."

We learn the art of making excuses early in life. Sometimes I think that this craft is actually innate. As soon as my daughter had command of the English language, excuses became a weapon of choice in her arsenal. Often I would ask my daughter to perform a task, only to find her response to be, "But Mommy, I'm tired." Or, "Mommy, I'm hungry." Or better yet, "Mommy, I have to finish my baby doll's hair. Then, I can do it. OK?"

Ironically, she really thought those excuses were sufficient enough for her to not do what I had asked her to.

As adults in relationship with our heavenly Father, we are no strangers to the art of excuse-making. We're just more sophisticated. Perhaps you think you need to first be married, or be unmarried, go to seminary, or wait until the children leave home.

There are many things in life that appear legitimate enough to cause us to want to delay in obeying what God has given us to do in life. God does not say that these other things are illegitimate—He is just not limited by them. And by His grace, neither are you. With God, all things are possible. No excuse is ever higher or more compelling than the will of God. Begin obeying God now, where you are, little by little, and you will be amazed at what you can accomplish.

> *"And another of his disciples said unto him, 'Lord, suffer me first to go and bury my father.' But Jesus said unto him, 'Follow me; and let the dead bury the dead.'"*
>
> (Matthew 8:21-22 KJV)

Prayer: Forgive me for not obeying you sooner. I make a commitment this day to begin obeying. I desire your will for my life. I will no longer make excuses.

Lesson Application

Date: _____

Today I will:

_____

_____

_____

_____

_____

_____

_____

Progress Made/Prayer Answered:

Date: _____

_____

_____

_____

_____

_____

_____

"You're not big like my Daddy!"

One day while in the kitchen my daughter came up to me and said, "You're not big like my Daddy!" She said in a teasing tone of voice.

"See…" she said, and pulled her daddy beside me so she could prove her point.

"No, Mommy is not as big as Daddy," I replied.

She smiled and went about her business. On many other occasions she noted how Daddy has big muscles and is big and strong. These attributes were appealing to her and helped make her feel safe.

The pride that my three-year-old had in having a big, strong daddy is the same pride we should take in our Father. We should be just as eager to size up the enemy in our lives.

"Look, I don't care what you bring my way, my Daddy is bigger than you," should be our response. First John 4:4 tells us, "Greater is He that is in us than He that is in the world."

God is bigger than everything this world brings—heartache, disappointment, pain, confusion, destruction, stress, fear. God is sovereign and nothing gets past Him. So, if it is in your life, you can get through it. Don't ever forget that the God we serve is the same God that delivered the Israelites, parted the Red Sea, healed the sick and resurrected the dead. He will deliver you too!

"For the eyes of the Lord run to and fro throughout the whole earth, to show himself strong on behalf of them whose heart is perfect toward him…"
(2 Chronicles 16:9 KJV)

Prayer: Lord, I thank you for being bigger than everything that comes my way. I will trust you and lean on you to get me through. Thank you for showing yourself strong on my behalf.

Lesson Application

Date: _____

Today I will:

_____

_____

_____

_____

_____

_____

_____

Progress Made/Prayer Answered:

Date: _____

_____

_____

_____

_____

_____

_____

"See, I can do it by myself now."

One morning my daughter ran up to me excitedly and said, "See Mommy, I can do it by myself now!" She was referring to her hair. She had spent a good amount of time creating those ponytails and putting colorful barrettes throughout.

Eager for my approval, I grinned and said, "Yes, honey you can do your hair by yourself. I'll just touch it up a little before we go."

"No, Mommy, I did it already," was her response.

My daughter was very happy that she could brush her hair and create her own ponytails. Children need and desire independence. From the moment they are born they are growing increasingly less dependent upon us. Not so with God. As Christians, we never grow independent of God. In fact, each day we must grow increasingly more dependent upon God. Daily our aim is to believe God more, trust God more, know God better, and yield to Him more fully. We never graduate from being a disciple of Christ.

When I was in college there were many students that would get degree after degree and never permanently matriculate from the university. We called such individuals perpetual students. Likewise, as Christians we must give into the fact that we are perpetual students of Christ. As much as we may want independence, God will always be there instructing, helping, and giving approval. We will never, ever matriculate out of God's school of life-long learning.

"Shew me thy ways, O Lord; teach me thy paths."
(Psalm 25:4-5 KJV)

Prayer: Lord, I am honored to be a disciple in the world's most prestigious institution of higher learning—yours. Help me this day to become more dependent upon you. I will study, listen, learn and obey.

Lesson Application

Date: _____

Today I will:

_____

_____

_____

_____

_____

_____

Progress Made/Prayer Answered:

Date: _____

_____

_____

_____

_____

_____

_____

"Where are
we going today?"

It's 7:00 A.M. One by one my family is awakening from sweet slumber. Out of the silence comes the first question of the day.

"Mommy, where are we going today?" my three-year-old asks.

To avoid having to answer a series of follow-up questions many times I would answer, "I don't know, sweetheart. As soon as I figure it out I'll let you know."

Our eyes were barely open and she was already seeking direction for her day. Of course I thought about myself. That is how the Lord wants us to be. "Lord, what would you have for me today?"

In Psalms 63, David said, "Lord thou art my God, early will I seek Thee…" God's plan for us is specific. God blesses us with talents and gifts, and plants thoughts and desires in our hearts. Often we may have a vision of our future, but we must seek Him daily to get detailed directions for the journey.

Proverbs, chapter 16, has many verses that describe how we work together with God to fulfill our purpose in life. Verse one tells us that we plan, but the ultimate answer comes from the Lord. Verse nine tells us that we plan, but the Lord directs our steps and makes them sure. In verse 25, we learn that ultimately there is a way that seems right to us but it ends in death and destruction. Thus, it is not only important to do God's will, but to do things God's way. By seeking God's direction each day, we ensure that we are going in the right direction.

> *"Roll your works upon the Lord [commit and trust them wholly to Him; He will cause your thoughts to become agreeable to His will, and] so shall your plans be established and succeed."*
>
> (Proverbs 16:3 AMP)

Prayer: Lord, Thou art my God. Early will I seek thee. I submit my thoughts and plans to you today. Direct my steps.

Lesson Application

Date: _____

Today I will:

_____

_____

_____

_____

_____

_____

Progress Made/Prayer Answered:

Date: _____

_____

_____

_____

_____

_____

_____

"Can we move to the next house like my friend?

One of my daughter's friends had recently moved into a larger, new home. So one morning my daughter asked me, "Mommy, can we move into the next house? A big house with a swing?"

"Yes," I answered, "one day we'll move into a larger home, but we can put a swing in our current backyard. We will put one up next summer."

"OK!" she said happily. It did not take long for me to discern what my daughter was really after. She was not after the larger home, she was after the wooden swing set in the backyard.

There are times when we as adults have difficulty discerning what it is we are really after.

*If only I was married…*you think. When really what you are after is unconditional love and companionship. The purist expression of love and acceptance comes from God. If you take the time to experience true communion with God you will find yourself complete and whole in Him alone.

The next time you find yourself wanting something, take a moment to discern what it is you are really longing for. Pray and ask God what you really need. God, through His word is the ultimate discerner of the thoughts and intents of the heart. He will lead you to true fulfillment and contentment.

"For the word of God is quick and powerful [living and active], and sharper than any two-edged sword, piercing even to the dividing asunder of soul and spirit and of the joints and marrow, and is a discerner of [quick to discern] the thoughts and intents of the heart."

(Hebrews 4:12 KJV)

Prayer: Lord, help me to discern your good, acceptable and perfect will for my life. Grant me the strength to resist the temptation to succumb to less than your best for me.

Lesson Application

Date: _____

Today I will:

_____

_____

_____

_____

_____

_____

_____

Progress Made/Prayer Answered:

Date: _____

_____

_____

_____

_____

_____

_____

"Mommy, where are you going?"

It's 5:00 A.M. I'm attempting to get up extra early to have my quiet time, only to have my three-year-old awaken seconds after me.

"Mommy, where are you going?" she asks.

It was one of those times when I definitely felt crowded. Never a moment alone—no matter how early I started. I told her I was going downstairs to have my quiet time and I asked her to stay in bed. Moments later she was downstairs on the couch beside me. Initially I was very frustrated

Then I prayed for a better attitude, strength to endure and the ability to accomplish what I needed—regardless. I decided to view it as a training opportunity. One day when she's an adult she will remember the discipline of rising early to seek the Lord. It was a positive legacy in the making that could have been ruined if I had a bad attitude towards her every time I got up for my special quiet time with God.

It is our responsibility to train our children in the way they should go—generally and specifically. Generally, we are to train them to know, love and follow Christ. Specifically, we are to help them discover and develop their gifts and talents, as well as their purpose in life and pursue it. That is the incredible task God has given us to do by His grace. This training is not accomplished through our Christian service or anything extraordinary but through our moment-by-moment walk with God before our children in the ordinary situations of life.

"You shall teach them diligently to your children, and shall talk of them when you sit in your house, when you walk by the way, when you lie down, and when you rise up."

(Deuteronomy 6:7 NKJV)

Prayer: Lord, help me to set a positive Christian example before my children at all times. Help me to overcome my shortcomings in order to exemplify Christ-like behavior that you will be proud of and that my children will grow to emulate.

Lesson Application

Date: _____

Today I will:

_____

_____

_____

_____

_____

_____

_____

Progress Made/Prayer Answered:

Date: _____

_____

_____

_____

_____

_____

_____

"I want to take a bath."

I was exhausted. It was one of those evenings when I just wanted to get the children in bed so I could go to bed.

"Mommy, I want to take a bath," my three-year-old said.

I realized then that avoiding the bath would probably require more effort than giving one, so I succumbed.

"Okay, but let's make it quick," I said.

Finally, my two toddlers were in pajamas and tucked in bed. Before I could utter a sigh of relief... "Mommy, will you read us a Bible story?"

Children are creatures of habit. I was naïve to think that I could bypass our bedtime ritual. I learned that it was easier to adhere to our nightly routine than to disrupt it. I now know that good habits are helpful. Everyone knows what to expect and is more likely to cooperate.

What good spiritual habits have you formed? Do you make it a point to set aside time to seek the Lord each day and attend church each week? Have you made a habit of operating in the fruit of the Spirit—love, joy, peace, longsuffering, gentleness, goodness, faithfulness, meekness and self-control? If you have, you will find that when you neglect to do these things you are unsettled in your spirit. You know you have "missed" it somewhere and you inwardly long to get back on track. Don't let a day go by without asking forgiveness. Don't let good habits slip. Unlike us weary moms, God is never too tired to give us a bath.

> *"If we confess our sins, he is faithful and just to forgive us our sins and to cleanse us from all unrighteousness."*
>
> (1 John 1:9 KJV)

Prayer: Lord, I've missed it. I've not always kept the good habits that I should. Please forgive me and help me to maintain good spiritual habits that help me in my walk with you.

Lesson Application

Date: _____

Today I will:

_____

_____

_____

_____

_____

_____

_____

Progress Made/Prayer Answered:

Date: _____

_____

_____

_____

_____

_____

_____

"I have a whole bunch of Granddaddies!"

"God bless Granddaddy and God bless my other Granddaddy. God bless Great-Granddaddy and God bless my other Great-Granddaddy…"

As my daughter said her bedtime prayer she looked up with excitement as she suddenly realized, "I have a whole bunch of Granddaddies—and Papa is a Granddaddy too!"

It brought her a real sense of joy to know that she had that many "fathers" who loved her and to whom she belonged. She had a living heritage. As she grows up and begins to study their lives, she will discover just how much each of these men has played a role in who she is—how she is a part of their legacy.

Likewise, we have a legacy of faith passed down to us by our spiritual forefathers. Hebrews, chapters 11 and 12, demonstrate to us what we can learn from our spiritual fathers. By faith Abel gave God his very best; by faith Enoch pleased God; by faith Noah built an ark and saved mankind; by faith Abraham conceived a son and became the father of many nations; by faith Moses led the people across the Red Sea as on dry land. They were commended for their faith—being sure of what they hoped for and certain of what they did not see.

However, the Bible also tells us that each of them was still "living by faith" when they died. They died before experiencing all that God had promised them. Yet they passed on a legacy of faith that enabled their children and their children's children to experience what God promised generations earlier.

Are you establishing a legacy of faith for your future generations? Will we be able to review the chronicles of this time to discover that you were a woman of faith who maintained her trust and reliance on God in spite of ridicule, tragedy or persecution? Do you inspire faith in others? Will you die believing—whether or not you see all that you envisioned?

Throughout the scriptures the generations are always intertwined. The decisions you make in your generation affect your children in the next. Make a decision to be a woman who lives by faith. It is the best inheritance you will ever leave.

"…I have set before you life and death, blessings and curses. Now choose life, so that you and your children may live."

(Deuteronomy 30:19 NIV)

75

Prayer: Father, I thank you for the legacy of faith my spiritual forefathers and mothers left me. Help me to be a woman of great faith who places your Word above all else and leaves this legacy for my children.

Lesson Application

Date: _____

Today I will:

_____

_____

_____

_____

_____

_____

_____

Progress Made/Prayer Answered:

Date: _____

_____

_____

_____

_____

_____

_____

"Mommy, where are you?"

Whenever I was out of my children's sight they would come looking. I would make sure they were content in the family room watching their favorite movie and then set off for the living room for a few moments of quiet. Before long I could hear the pitter-patter of feet wandering into the room bringing their toys with them.

"Why are you in here?" I asked. "Your movie is on."

"I know," my three-year-old said, "But Mommy, it's okay…I'm in here now."

"I know, but Mommy is trying to read."

It was useless. No matter where I went in my home, my children were sure to follow. To their credit, however, very often they would sit quietly for mommy—content just to be in my presence.

In the book of Psalms, David admonishes us to seek this type of closeness and intimacy with our Father.

"Thou art my hiding place" (Psalm 32:5).

"My soul thirsteth for God" (Psalm42:2).

"My soul followeth hard after Thee" (Psalm 63:8).

The Bible makes it clear that the benefits of abiding in God's presence outweigh whatever sacrifices we have to make to get alone with Him—to get quiet before Him.

Psalm 16:11 tells us that "Thou will show me the path of life; in Thy presence is fullness of joy; at Thy right hand there are pleasures for evermore." Everything we need and desire is in God. Your strength, joy, inner peace, contentment and hope are all drawn from your intimacy with God.

> *"But it is good for me to draw near to God...."*
> (Psalm 73:28 KJV)

Prayer: Heavenly Father, I know that everything I need and desire in life is in you. Help me to draw nigh to you. I long to be in your presence.

Lesson Application

Date: _____

Today I will:

_____

_____

_____

_____

_____

_____

_____

Progress Made/Prayer Answered:

Date: _____

_____

_____

_____

_____

_____

_____

"Jesus died on the cross for us."

"TODAY?"

One morning my husband and I were teaching our three-year-old a song that demonstrates Jesus dying on the cross for us. When we concluded, I wanted to make sure she understood what we were singing about. So I said to her, "Jesus died on the cross for us." Suddenly, she looked up eagerly.

"Today?" she asked.

My husband and I got a really good giggle from that remark.

I said no, that it was many years ago, but it is just as good as if it were today.

I was quickly reminded of just how powerful Jesus' death and resurrection really was. Jesus was beaten, crucified, and rose again 2,000 years ago so that we could enjoy abundant life today.

As you embark upon the events of this day be reminded that because of Jesus you have peace, strength, victory over sin, purpose, everlasting life and intimacy with God. In fact, the Bible tells us that Christ's divine power has given us all things that pertain to life and godliness (2 Peter 1:3). So we can have full confidence that whatever we come up against, our Christian faith provides us with everything we need to be overcomers in life.

> *"For everyone born of God overcomes the world. This is the victory that has overcome the world, even our faith."*
>
> (1 John 5:4 NIV)

Prayer: Lord, I thank you for bearing my sins and dying on the cross for me. Because of you, I am an overcomer. I will overcome the challenges that confront me this day.

Lesson Application

Date: _____

Today I will:

_____

_____

_____

_____

_____

_____

_____

Progress Made/Prayer Answered:

Date: _____

_____

_____

_____

_____

_____

_____

"Mommy, do you want me to help with it?"

One afternoon I was sorting a large pile of towels and loading them into the washing machine. I was about seven months pregnant with my third child and feeling a bit encumbered by the task. My three-year-old daughter observed my plight and offered her assistance.

"Mommy, do you want me to help with it?"

The children's play room was adjacent to the laundry room and there was plenty for my daughter to do. Yet she wanted to see what I was doing and soon realized she could help.

"Sure, you can help," I said. I was surprised by and appreciative of her help. She did all the bending and carried all the towels to the washer. A big help she was.

In the midst of completing our daily to-do lists it is important for us to take a moment to identify with the work of our heavenly Father. While running from the grocer, to the pediatrician, to the dry cleaners, be mindful of the individuals the Lord places within your path. Everyone you "run into" you encounter for a reason. What kind word, or word of comfort or wisdom might you be able to share with someone? Recognize that this is the real reason you interact with people.

The work of our heavenly Father is to draw all men, women, boys and girls unto Himself. He does not want anyone to perish. So He's given us the shared responsibility to help Him reach those who are lost and hurting. God cannot save the world by Himself. He needs us to be His hands, His feet and His voice to all those with whom we come in contact.

> *"For we are God's fellow workers, you are God's field, God's building"*
>
> (1 Corinthians 3:9 NIV)

Prayer: Lord, please help me to recognize and seize every opportunity to be a blessing to others whether it is in word or in deed. Help me to help you draw others unto yourself; remembering that is my true Christian service.

Lesson Application

Date: _____

Today I will:

_____

_____

_____

_____

_____

_____

_____

Progress Made/Prayer Answered:

Date: _____

_____

_____

_____

_____

_____

_____

"I don't want to be different."

I was getting my daughter dressed for preschool one day when she vehemently opposed wearing the pretty dress I laid out for her.

"But I don't want to wear a dress. I want to wear pants! Everybody wears pants."

She happened to love pretty dresses but had become influenced by the fact that most of the other girls wore pants to school most days.

"It's good to be different," I told her. But she wasn't convinced. She simply wanted to be inconspicuous and blend in with the other girls.

How often do we as Christians just want to be inconspicuous and blend into our surroundings? We would rather not cause a fuss. However that scenario is not always possible. Often when we stand up for what we believe to be true, we are opposed. In

2 Timothy 3:12, Jesus forewarned us that we would suffer persecution for righteousness' sake (doing the right thing).

I recall many sneers and unkind words spoken to me when I gave my life to Christ back in college. Many of my friends thought I had "lost it" and had gone way overboard because of the drastic changes I made in my life. I accepted Christ as my Lord and made a decision to yield my will to Him. I quickly discovered that how He would have me live my life was very different from the way I had been living it on my own. Some of my friends did not appreciate the change because they felt they were being judged by my new lifestyle. I did not set out to make myself different, I just set out to follow Christ.

I am reminded of a phrase I once heard from Bible teacher Chuck Swindoll and I've never forgotten it. His words were simply, "Obey God and leave the consequences to Him."

> *"But you are a chosen people, a royal priesthood, a holy nation, a people belonging to God, that you may declare the praises of him who called you out of darkness into his wonderful light."*
>
> (1 Peter 2:9 NIV)

Prayer: Heavenly Father, help me to stand up for righteousness even if it means being different. I will obey you and leave the consequences to you.

Lesson Application

Date: _____

Today I will:

_____

_____

_____

_____

_____

_____

_____

Progress Made/Prayer Answered:

Date: _____

_____

_____

_____

_____

_____

_____

"I want to do all that stuff."

When my daughter was four she attended preschool on Monday, Wednesday and Friday. On Tuesday we attended story time at the library. On Wednesday (our busiest day) after school she attended ballet class. Then, we would eat on the road and make our way to church that evening. My daughter loved Wednesdays. She liked to stay on the go.

One morning she said to me, "Mommy, I want to go to school, ballet, the playground, story time—I want to do all that stuff!" The idea of doing all of the things she liked in one day was very appealing to her.

I'm no different. I want everything to happen now as well. If I'm honest, I would love to have the full fruition of my and my husband's vision today— the big business, the dream home, fully funded college tuition for our children, extended exotic vacations, etc. Yet as much as we want it all to happen now, I'm learning that we have to take life in stages and build upon each new step we take. We don't fulfill our purpose in a day. I am beginning to understand *why* things take time.

Setting and working toward goals is good for our physical and faith muscles. Attaining goals is very rewarding and further builds our faith and confidence. Throughout God's Word, He is very clear that He intends for us to increase in everything progressively, decently and in order, in His timing and on the path He has for us. When we do, we get God's very best and the fruit of it is exceedingly sweet.

So don't be anxious for the full manifestation of your life's vision. Enjoy the journey and extract all that you can out of every precious moment along the way.

> *"To every thing there is a season, and a time to every purpose under the heaven…"*
>
> (Ecclesiastes 3:1 KJV)

Prayer: Lord, I thank you that you're walking with me and guiding me as I seek to fulfill my purpose in life. By your grace I will fulfill my life's purpose step-by-step, enjoying the journey along the way.

Lesson Application

Date: _____

Today I will:

_____

_____

_____

_____

_____

_____

_____

Progress Made/Prayer Answered:

Date: _____

_____

_____

_____

_____

_____

_____

"I don't want to dream anymore."

One night my daughter had a bad dream. That next morning she told me that she didn't want to dream anymore. That night during our bedtime prayer I had her repeat after me that her sleep would be sweet and that she would have only good dreams. She fell fast asleep.

The words of my toddler's statement were so very poignant to me. "I don't want to dream anymore." Of course she meant it literally, but I thought, "How incredibly devastating for one to not want to dream anymore." If we cannot dream, what are we living for? That is why it is critical that we know Jesus, who is the source of our hope.

Because Jesus faced and conquered the ultimate in death, we have hope that through Him we can also overcome anything. Because we know God is with us and wants the best for us, we have hope that all things really will work together for good. As a result of knowing Jesus intimately we can have the dream God wants us to have and keep that dream alive no matter what we face.

On the road to fulfilling our life's dreams we inevitably encounter excruciating experiences and roadblocks, but we cannot allow ourselves to stop dreaming. Do whatever you have to do to maintain your hope. Immerse yourself in God's Word. Pray, seek help, stir up the gift and renew that dream within you.

"Where there is no vision the people perish..."
(Proverbs 29:18 KJV)

Prayer: Lord, there are times when I feel as though I want to give up. Please help me to keep my faith and confidence in you. I trust that you are working everything together for good. I will continue to dream. I will keep hope alive.

Lesson Application

Date: _____

Today I will:

_____

_____

_____

_____

_____

_____

_____

Progress Made/Prayer Answered:

Date: _____

_____

_____

_____

_____

_____

_____

"But I don't want to eat food."

On the way home from preschool my daughter wanted to stop for ice cream. I told her she had to eat food first and that food makes us healthy and strong. "But I don't want to eat food," was her response.

Ideally, we would love for life to be full of ice cream (or a bowl of cherries). But good times alone do not make us spiritually healthy and strong. It's the fine balance of good/restful times along with trials, tribulations, affliction and persecution that make and mold us into the strong, healthy, overcomers God wants us to be. Only God our Father knows our recommended daily allowance of the various spiritual food groups.

Although we would love to live off sweets alone, too much sugar will cause us to be rotten—like a "spoiled rotten" child—selfish, insensitive, self-righteous, without compassion, judgmental. That is what happens to us as Christians without a salty or sour experience to balance our diet and help humble us. We all know that dark, leafy vegetables are filled with nutrients. Similarly, the dark times in our lives can help bring forth our very best and help develop us into individuals we did not even know we were capable of becoming.

While we do not enjoy the darker seasons of life, we must remember that we will become better Christians, wives and mothers if we absorb the necessary vitamins and nutrients from all of life's experiences so that we can become healthy, strong believers.

> "A just balance and scales are the Lord's; all the weights of the bag are His work [established on His eternal principles]."
>
> (Proverbs 16:11 AMP)

Prayer: Dear Lord, please help me develop a spiritually balanced diet so that I can be the believer you intended me to be.

Lesson Application

Date: _____

Today I will:

_____

_____

_____

_____

_____

_____

_____

Progress Made/Prayer Answered:

Date: _____

_____

_____

_____

_____

_____

_____

"I want money."

"I want money, Mommy!" My two-year-old son exclaimed after desperately searching his pants pockets. As it turned out, he had plenty of money, he just couldn't get it out of his deep pockets. I guess he thought it would be easier to just ask me for more money. But I encouraged him to dig deep.

"Keep trying," I said.

About 15 seconds later he said, "I got my money, Mommy" and walked away content. He had the money he wanted in his possession the entire time.

I do not know many people who cannot identify with the phrase "I want money." Money is very useful for so many things on this earth, and our natural/physical lives are made easier by the conveniences money is able to buy. However, like my two-year-old son, we often pray to God to give us money when God is looking at us saying, "What have I already given you? Dig deep."

We have to put forth some creative energy, but Scripture tells us that God has given us the power to create wealth (Deuteronomy 8:18). Second Kings, chapter 4, describes a woman whose husband died and left her deep in debt. Her husband's creditors had come to take her two sons as slaves. She was in desperate need for money and cried out to the prophet Elisha. In turn Elisha asked if she had anything of value in her house. She had one jar of oil. The prophet gave her specific instructions which she followed. The jar of oil was multiplied to the point where she could sell the oil, pay off her debt and live off the rest.

God intends for us to use the gifts, talents and resources with which He has blessed us to create the wealth we need. Like the widow in 2 Kings, we have in "seed form" what we need to prosper financially. What gift has God given you? What idea do you have that needs to be acted upon in faith? If you don't know, ask God to show you (and your husband). The provision for your family is within your family. Believe the Word of God that comes to you and act on it.

> *"But remember the LORD your God, for it is he who gives you the ability to produce wealth, and so confirms his covenant, which he swore to your forefathers, as it is today."*
>
> (Deuteronomy 8:18 NIV)

Prayer: Lord, I thank you for the unique gifts and talents you have placed in me and my family. Please show us how to utilize these gifts in a way that will glorify you and bring the financial provision you have promised.

Lesson Application

Date: _____

Today I will:

_____

_____

_____

_____

_____

_____

_____

Progress Made/Prayer Answered:

Date: _____

_____

_____

_____

_____

_____

_____

"I don't want to wear that."

Every morning I would lay out my three-year-old daughter's clothes for her. But as she progressed throughout her year as a three-year-old, the more resistance I got. Then I began allowing her to select her own clothes to wear each morning. Yet often she would dilly-dally around and not select anything. So, I would choose something for her.

But then she'd say, "I don't want to wear that."

If she had two outfits left in the drawer and I chose one, she would select the other. At other times, she would not want to choose from among the available options. She would want to wear something that was dirty and needed to be washed.

Apparently my three-year-old had her own idea of how she wanted to look, and often it was different than mine. I encourage self-expression, but with limits—one being that the clothes she wears are clean.

In God's Word, He lays out the clothes He would like us to wear. Colossians, chapter 3, says that if we are risen with Christ, we should take off our old clothes (anger, wrath, malice, slander, and filthy language) and put on the clothes of God's chosen people—compassion, kindness, humility, gentleness, patience, forgiveness, love and peace (Colossians 3:12-15).

Of course the challenge we face is that the clothes God wants us to wear aren't the trendiest, nor do they make the hottest fashion statement. But they protect us, they keep us warm, they're clean, and they are an eternal investment in our future—they never go out of style. So, make a commitment to permanently trade in your old clothes and old way of thinking and acting for the priceless designer clothes God has for us.

> *"Therefore, as God's chosen people, holy and dearly loved, clothe yourselves, with compassion, kindness, humility, gentleness and patience."*
> (Colossians 3:12 NIV)

Prayer: Dear Lord, help me to appreciate the wonderful signature apparel you have designed for me. I will create new trends and influence others by boldly wearing the designs you've created for me.

Lesson Application

Date: _____

Today I will:

_____

_____

_____

_____

_____

_____

_____

Progress Made/Prayer Answered:

Date: _____

_____

_____

_____

_____

_____

_____

"But I am still little."

It was bedtime. My two-year-old had fallen asleep on the couch and I decided to carry him upstairs to his room. His older sister saw me carrying him and wanted me to carry her to bed too.

I said to her, "He's a *little* boy. You're a *big* girl."

Contrary to her typical proclamations she stated, "But I *am* still little."

"Oh," I said. Typically, if anyone ever refers to her as a "cute little girl" or "a little sweetheart," she swiftly corrects them by saying, "I'm not a little girl; I'm a big girl!"

This time however, in order for her to have her need met the way she wanted it, it was convenient for her to be a little girl.

Honestly, we're not so different than our little/big girls. There are times when we make decisions without consulting God because we're *big* girls. At the same time, let something difficult or disappointing occur and we humble ourselves at the feet of God.

"God, I just can't do this. I can't take this anymore. Please, help me!" says the *little* girl within us.

The reality is, we are to always remain humble and child-like before God. We are to seek God in every situation. We can't live submitted to God as a child one moment, and act like an equal *to* God the next. We are and will forever be God's beloved children.

> "The Spirit Himself bears witness with our spirit that we are children of God."
> (Romans 8:16 NKJV)

Prayer: Dear Lord, please help me to remain as a child before you who continually seeks your guidance and your help. I want to grow more and more dependent upon you.

Lesson Application

Date: _____

Today I will:

_____

_____

_____

_____

_____

_____

_____

Progress Made/Prayer Answered:

Date: _____

_____

_____

_____

_____

_____

_____

"Nobody can scratch my back."

While driving on the highway one evening, my daughter got a terrible itch on her back. She squirmed and grunted for a moment and finally blurted out, "Nobody can scratch my back! My brother can't do it because he's strapped in. Mommy you can't do it because you're driving...Mom, it itches!"

Feeling her agony I came up with a creative idea. I reached back and handed her a comb from out of my purse and told her to use it to scratch her back. It worked. She was able to scratch her back herself and it brought her and the rest of us much comfort.

When my daughter first got her itch, her initial response was to look for someone who could come to her rescue—someone who could scratch her back. As adults, when we're in a bind, we often look first to others to help aid or rescue us. You may feel there is no one to pray with you, listen to you or encourage you.

The Bible tells us that when David and his army in the Bible had just lost everything to an enemy—their wives, children and possessions—they were very distraught. Everyone was discouraged and there was no one to encourage anyone. As the leader, David had to pull himself together. Scripture tells us that "David encouraged himself in the Lord" (1 Samuel 30:6).

David asked the Lord what to do and then obeyed. When you're at your wits end, before you grab the phone to call that trusted friend or family member, take some time to encourage yourself. Tell the Lord all about it. Ask Him what you ought to do and then obey.

"In the world ye shall have tribulation, but be of good cheer; I have overcome the world."
(John 16:33 KJV)

Prayer: Dear Lord, I thank you that you are always with me even when others are not. No matter how devastating the problem is, I will look to your Word and encourage myself.

Lesson Application

Date: _____

Today I will:

_____

_____

_____

_____

_____

_____

_____

Progress Made/Prayer Answered:

Date: _____

_____

_____

_____

_____

_____

_____

"I want you to do it."

It is time to put her shoes on and my four-year-old insists she cannot do it.

"I want you to do it," she says. Now this is something she is totally capable of doing but she does not want to take on the responsibility to get it done.

While I was not happy with her decision to act inept as it related to the simple act of putting on her shoes, I could empathize with her. There are a lot of things in life that (if I am honest about it) I wish God would just do for me. Like, instantly take off these extra pounds I'm carrying or bless me with perfect love and perfect patience. Life would certainly be easier if God would do these things for me.

However, I am fully capable of eating right, exercising, and nurturing the fruit of love and patience. But it takes work and effort. It's called spiritual growth. God wants us to take on more and more responsibility for ourselves and use what He has given us to do it. Through Jesus Christ He has given us His word, His power and His authority. We just have to supply the will power. What areas of your life are you wishing God would miraculously rectify for you? Know that you can be who God has purposed for you to be and with God's help you do have the ability to make the changes necessary to get there.

"His divine power has given us everything we need for life and godliness through our knowledge of Him who called us by His own glory and goodness."
(2 Peter 1:3 NIV)

Prayer: Heavenly Father, please help me to grow up in the areas of my life for which I've taken too little responsibility. I know that your divine power has given me everything I need for life and godliness and I will no longer make excuses. I will utilize the power you have given me to become the woman you have purposed for me.

Lesson Application

Date: _____

Today I will:

_____

_____

_____

_____

_____

_____

_____

Progress Made/Prayer Answered:

Date: _____

_____

_____

_____

_____

_____

_____

"But I'm really tired..."

When it is time to clean up at the end of the day, my son or daughter will usually say, "But I'm really tired"—as if being tired will relinquish them from the responsibility of cleaning up.

You know, many days I'm just tired. Tired of getting up (for middle-of-the-night feedings), tired of cleaning up the house, picking up after little ones, washing dishes, washing clothes and dirty faces, sweeping up after each meal and snack, and folding up all those miniature clothing items—especially matching the socks. I just want to relax. Sit down. Read a magazine. Take a bath. Read a book. Talk on the phone uninterrupted. Take a walk along the lake. Or if I'm really fortunate—go to the spa.

But life just isn't set up that way. Unless you can afford to hire someone to do the things for which you are responsible, you are required to do them. And you know what, you can do them—and with joy. God has made us by nature to be responsible individuals. God gave Adam a beautiful garden—heaven on earth—but he had to tend to it. He was responsible for it. Likewise, God has given us beautiful blessings straight from heaven (called children) for which we are responsible and which we can handle.

So the next time you are tired of getting up, cleaning up, picking up and just feel like giving up, start looking up—to the author and perfecter of your faith. He will refresh your weary soul, endow you with strength, and remind you of just how important and rewarding the task of rearing responsible, God-loving children really is.

> *"...And let us run with perseverance the race marked out for us. Let us fix our eyes on Jesus, the author and perfecter of our faith, who for the joy set before him endured the cross, scorning its shame, and sat down at the right hand of the throne of God"*
>
> (Hebrews 12:1b-2 NIV)

Prayer: Holy Spirit, help me to put my daily tasks into the proper perspective. Help me to remember that you have called, appointed and anointed me for this ministry of mothering. I will perform my duties "as unto you" Lord, with joy and cheerfulness of heart.

Lesson Application

Date: _____

Today I will:

_____

_____

_____

_____

_____

_____

_____

Progress Made/Prayer Answered:

Date: _____

_____

_____

_____

_____

_____

_____

"But Mommy, I want to talk to you."

So, my four-year-old daughter is already exhibiting signs of being a *bona fide* female. I am busy trying to pay some bills or do something else I have difficulty getting to.

"But Mommy, I want to talk to you," my daughter interrupts.

"I'll be done shortly; just wait, honey," I replied.

Just wait. Aren't you glad that when we come to God He never says, "I'll be with you momentarily. Just wait." My goodness, most of us wait until the last minute to come to God anyway. If He had us wait before hearing our request we probably wouldn't survive.

Fortunately for us, God is omnipresent and ready, willing and able to hear and respond to the myriad of requests from each individual on this planet. God really does care about what you are going through. Jesus Christ lived on earth as a man and endured trouble, trials and temptations just as we do. Jesus does not look down on us in a judging manner. The Bible says that when Jesus saw the people, He was moved with compassion because they were distressed and helpless (Matthew 9:36). Scripture doesn't say He looks upon them in disgust because they were distressed and helpless. Jesus came to help and he has sent the Holy Spirit to help you too.

So don't put off calling God for help. There is no annoying sequence of automated prompts and you won't be put on hold. With God you are always the first in line.

> *"Therefore I will look unto the Lord; I will wait for the God of my salvation: my God will hear me."*
> (Micah 7:7 KJV)

Prayer: Lord, I come to you. I will talk honestly and openly. I know that your willingness and ability to hear and respond to me is far more than any human. Therefore, I look to you as my source. Thank you for always having a listening ear, and for giving me the perfect solution to every dilemma.

Lesson Application

Date: _____

Today I will:

_____

_____

_____

_____

_____

_____

_____

Progress Made/Prayer Answered:

Date: _____

_____

_____

_____

_____

_____

_____

"That's mine!"

We're in the car. My daughter has run out of juice and her brother has barely touched his. She's still thirsty and I suggest that my son share with his sister.

"That's mine!" he says.

It seemed as though he got pleasure out of having something she did not have and he didn't want to yield. I tried to stress the importance of sharing (to a two-year-old). Then, I realized that he didn't recognize the source of the juice he had. I was the one who gave him the juice and I was asking him to share it. I tried to let him know that there was more where that came from. He didn't relent. Eventually I just took the cup and gave it to his sister. She took a sip and gave it back.

What an eye-opener that experience was for me. Now I see why God is so enthusiastic about our sharing what we have with others. Whatever we have He has given us. If we have a brother, sister, friend or stranger in need, we should willingly share of our abundance. Why? Well, there is more where that came from. If we use our resources and we begin to run low, God will give us more. If my son had shared his juice with his sister and she drank it all, I would have given him more. God is no different.

On the other hand, if we're selfish, we'll find things being "taken" from us. We won't be able to keep what we have, and even when we get more it will vanish away. Funny how that works, but it's God's way. If we are generous, cheerful givers—to God first and others second—we will always have what we need.

> *"Give and it will be given to you. A good measure, pressed down, shaken together and running over, will be poured into your lap. For with the measure you use, it will be measured to you."*
>
> (Luke 6:38 NIV)

Prayer: Lord, forgive me for my selfishness. Help me to give liberally to you first, as well as to those in need that through my generosity others might be drawn to you.

Lesson Application

Date: _____

Today I will:

_____

_____

_____

_____

_____

_____

Progress Made/Prayer Answered:

Date: _____

_____

_____

_____

_____

_____

_____

"Is it morning time yet?"

On cloudy mornings when there is some light in the sky but the sun is not shining, my children often ask, "Is it morning time yet?"

They are anxious to get out of bed and begin their day. They are hoping I won't tell them, "No it's still nighttime. Get back in bed." They don't like bedtime and nighttime. They much prefer the excitement and thrills of daytime...

Don't we all. Have you ever been in a season of nighttime that seemed to last forever? Is there some light, but no bright, warm, cheerful sunlight? Do you find yourself asking the Lord, "Is it morning time yet?"—time to get up out of this situation that has been a thorn in my side for far too long? Join the crowd.

Jesus promised His disciples that in this life they would have tribulation. In addition, most of us will have our own "wilderness" experience just as the children of Israel did. We'll wander around through something for years or decades although it could have been dealt with in weeks or months. In the meantime, we must trust God, be willing and obedient, have faith and patience, and we will inherit the promise. Hang in there. Morning is coming.

> *"...Weeping may endure for a night, but joy comes in the morning."*
>
> (Psalm 30:5b KJV)

Prayer: Lord, sometimes I so want to be delivered of this thing that burdens me. Help me to keep the faith. I know that with you all things are possible and I just have to be patient. I rejoice now that my morning is coming.

Lesson Application

Date: _____

Today I will:

_____

_____

_____

_____

_____

_____

_____

Progress Made/Prayer Answered:

Date: _____

_____

_____

_____

_____

_____

_____

"I don't want stock in my Malt-O-Meal."

When my first two children were ages three and two, they thoroughly enjoyed a good, hot bowl of Malt-O-Meal. It happened to be one of my husband's favorite breakfast cereals growing up and it became my children's as well.

It got to the point where all they wanted to eat for breakfast was Malt-O-Meal. Soon, we were emptying a box about every two weeks. One morning as expected, my daughter approached my husband and said, "Daddy, I want Malt-O-Meal…"

My husband, recognizing just how much money we were investing in this particular brand of hot cereal, thought out loud, "As much as you eat this cereal, we need to get you some stock in Malt-O-Meal!"

Immediately my daughter looked up at her daddy with a bewildered look on her face and said, "But Daddy, I don't want stock in my Malt-O-Meal."

My husband and I burst into laughter. He was referring to purchasing monetary shares of the company that manufactures Malt-O-Meal for a long-term investment, and my daughter literally thought he was suggesting that we put "stock" in her favorite morning cereal. She clearly liked her Malt-O-Meal the way it was and had no interest in tampering with it—especially with "stock."

I couldn't help but think that just how my daughter sounded so funny to me and my husband, we must sound this way to God sometimes. The Bible tells us that His thoughts are not our thoughts and His ways are not our ways, for His thoughts are higher than our thoughts and His ways higher than our ways.

God may tell us He wants to accomplish something in our lives that could be very fruitful and beneficial to us and others, but we cannot even comprehend what He is recommending. That is why the Bible tells us to renew our minds. If we fail to put on the mind of Christ, we may miss what God is trying to do in our lives and say no to our heavenly Father when He tries to bless us.

"Do not conform any longer to the pattern of this world, but be transformed by the renewing of your mind. Then you will be able to test and approve what God's will is—his good, pleasing and perfect will."

(Romans 12:2 NIV)

Prayer: Lord, I desire to know and understand your good, pleasing and perfect will for my life. I acknowledge that your thoughts are higher than my thoughts and your ways are higher than my ways and I will daily renew my mind in your Word.

Lesson Application

Date: _____

Today I will:

_____

_____

_____

_____

_____

_____

_____

Progress Made/Prayer Answered:

Date: _____

_____

_____

_____

_____

_____

_____

"Why do you have to be the Mommy?"

You should wear a sweater," I said to my four-year-old while she was getting dressed.

I was advising her to put on a sweater because it was going to be a cold day. But she didn't want to wear a sweater. She wanted to wear lightweight clothes. She had in mind what she wanted to wear and did not appreciate my overriding her decision.

"Why do you have to be the mommy? I wish I was *your* mommy," she said to me. It was clear that she would much rather be the one giving the directives instead of receiving them.

As I reflected on her comment I couldn't help but identify with her statement. I guess I kind of feel that way, too—towards God.

Why do you have to be the God? I wish I was God. In other words, why can't I make the decisions and do what *I* want to do? Why do I have to submit *my* will to God's will? It seems as though life would be much easier (or at least more fun) if I was responsible for being God.

The truth is, life would not be easier nor more fun if I was in charge. God is all-knowing and infinitely more wise and powerful. He has the best, and only, qualifications for the job. If I held the position of God in my life I would surely be in trouble. Like my daughter and her clothing decisions, I would be ignorantly stepping out into a cold world wearing only a T-shirt. I would be unwarned, ill-prepared and in for a harsh reality check.

When we take the time to listen to God and take His directives, He helps us lead the most fruitful and peace-filled life. Be assured that in this world you will have tribulation, but if you allow yourself to take direction from God, you will surely have fewer of those painful, self-inflicted tribulations.

> *"Look to Me, and be saved, all you ends of the earth!*
> *For I am God, and there is no other."*
> (Isaiah 45:22 NKJV)

Prayer: Dear Lord, truly there are times when I wish I was in control. But I realize it is vanity. Please help me yield to your infinite wisdom. You know what's best for me.

Lesson Application

Date: _____

Today I will:

_____

_____

_____

_____

_____

_____

_____

Progress Made/Prayer Answered:

Date: _____

_____

_____

_____

_____

_____

_____

"My stomach is growling."

M ommy, my stomach is growling." Those were the words I could expect to hear each morning if my two and a half year old hadn't eaten by 8:00 A.M. No matter how much I may have wanted to stay in my bed, I knew I had to get up and prepare breakfast or it was all downhill from there. My son would only get more impatient, more irritable, and more difficult to tolerate.

I guess the good thing is that he knew and was able to communicate when he was hungry. At that point it was my responsibility to meet that need.

God expects the same from us. We ought to recognize when we are spiritually hungry. Impatience, irritability, difficulty tolerating and being tolerated by others is a sure-fire sign that we need to ingest more fruit of the Spirit. We shouldn't go days, weeks and months without spiritual nourishment. But if we have, the most important thing we can do is acknowledge that we are hungry and need to be fed. We must go to our source for our supply. No one or nothing else can serve as a suitable substitute for our spiritual hunger. Only God and His Word will meet that need.

So go ahead, tell God you're hungry.

"Blessed are those who hunger and thirst for righteousness, for they will be filled."
(Matthew 5:6 NIV)

Prayer: Dear Lord, I acknowledge that spiritually, I am hungry and in need of nourishment. Please feed me with your Word so that I may be strong, spiritually fit, and able to fulfill the abundant life you have for me.

Lesson Application

Date: _____

Today I will:

_____

_____

_____

_____

_____

_____

_____

Progress Made/Prayer Answered:

Date: _____

_____

_____

_____

_____

_____

_____

"Mommy, you do know."

My four-year-old daughter always expected me to have a ready answer for each of her many questions throughout the day. She thought very highly of me—as they all do at that age—and whenever I told her that I honestly did not have an answer, she would abruptly answer back.

"Mommy, you *do* know," she'd state.

"No, I'm sorry honey, but I really don't," I'd reply.

"Mommm…"

"I'm sorry to disappoint you baby, but I'm telling you the truth."

Many times we take just the opposite approach with God. We make requests or ask questions of God and, then, neglect to wait for the answer. We go ahead and do our *own* thing and make the decision *we* deem best. We say by our behavior that we don't really think He knows. But He *does* know. God knows the answer and holds the solution. And if we're sensitive to the Holy Spirit, God will lead us in just the right direction.

We may not like the answer we receive, but we can be assured that unlike us, God always has the answer for life's questions.

> *"He shall call upon Me, and I will answer him; I will be with him in trouble; I will deliver him and honor him."*
>
> (Psalm 91:15 NKJV)

Prayer: Dear Lord, I know you hold the answers and solutions to the challenges I face every day. Help me to draw near to you and truly listen with my heart. I expect to hear from you. I will hear and I will obey.

Lesson Application

Date: _____

Today I will:

_____

_____

_____

_____

_____

_____

_____

Progress Made/Prayer Answered:

Date: _____

_____

_____

_____

_____

_____

_____

"Mommy, you said that yesterday."

My four-year-old son guzzled down all of his 100% Florida orange juice at breakfast and then said he was too full to eat his cereal.

"Son, I'm not giving you anything to drink anymore. You must wait until after you finish eating," I said authoritatively.

Then my five-year-old daughter quickly reminded me, "Mom, you said that yesterday."

"Oh," I responded—slightly embarrassed.

I realized that it is much easier to talk a good game than it is to follow through. As mothers we respond to our young children so many times in a day that it is easy to forget what we have said. Fortunately, God has a much better memory than we. God never forgets His Word. Not only does He not forget what He has said but He promises to bring it to pass. He also has given us permission to "put Him in remembrance" of His Word.

If you have heard God speaking to you concerning a particular area of your life and it lines up with His written word, you can be assured that He will make good on his promise. Unlike a harried mom, He won't forget what he said and He also won't mind if you remind Him of His promise until it manifests in your life.

> *"What I have said, that will I bring about; what I have planned, that will I do."*
>
> (Isaiah 46:11 NIV)

Prayer: Lord, although I don't see everything you've promised coming to pass in my life right now, I know that it will in time. Help me to trust you more and more.

Lesson Application

Date: _____

Today I will:

_____

_____

_____

_____

_____

_____

Progress Made/Prayer Answered:

Date: _____

_____

_____

_____

_____

_____

_____

"I didn't ask for it."

My daughter ate her oatmeal and left her toast on the table.

"Mommy I don't want this toast. I didn't ask for it."

She likes toast. I assumed that she wanted it. I also assumed that even though she didn't want it she would eat it anyway— because I'd made it for her. However, she didn't ask for it. And, God is the same way.

We may not understand it, but God really only wants what He's asked from us. We can think we're the consummate saint by giving God all these seemingly wonderful things—like become a missionary to Africa or Asia—but if these things are not what God has asked of us, it won't count for much. He may accept it, but he may not be enthusiastic about it.

Just as our children choose to do the chores *they* want to do—although we've already assigned them a specific chore—they come back to us giddy about what they *did* do and we're appreciative but not enthusiastic. We had someone else for that job that may even have done a better job at it. We still want them to do what we asked *them* to do. Doing a good deed doesn't relieve us of our responsibility before God. Endeavor to do God's will.

"But you be watchful in all things, endure afflictions, do the work of an evangelist, fulfill your ministry."

(2 Timothy 4:5 NKJV)

Prayer: Lord, please help me to discern and engage in only the things you have ordained for me to do in life. I desire to please you.

Lesson Application

Date: _____

Today I will:

_____

_____

_____

_____

_____

_____

_____

Progress Made/Prayer Answered:

Date: _____

_____

_____

_____

_____

_____

_____

"I like to lie."

Are you lying to me?" My husband asked my three-year-old.

This odd conversation began after my daughter asked her dad for a snack. Her dad just told her she could have a snack *later*. But nevertheless, she kept responding,

"But, I want it now!" she blurted.

Then my husband finally asked her, "Did you hear what I said?"

And she responded, "No."

"Are you lying to me?" he asked firmly.

"Yes," she said sheepishly.

"Why?"

"Because, I like to lie."

Although my husband and I were not happy with her answer, we had to concede to the fact that at least she was honest. When Adam disobeyed God in the garden, Adam hid from God. God confronted him directly and Adam cast blame. Not this little girl. At least not in this instance.

The question is: would we consider being as honest? Only through complete honesty can God help us identify our shortcomings and then help craft us into better Christians.

My daughter admitted that it felt better to pretend not to hear what her father was saying than to adhere to the truth and risk not getting what she wanted. No, it wasn't the right thing to do. But, it was right for her to admit the truth once confronted.

The next time the Holy Spirit confronts you and convicts you of an attitude or action that is not pleasing to God, take a deep breath and when God asks why, just admit it.

"Because I like it, God..." As difficult as it may be to admit it, if it's the truth, say so. That confession may be the very thing you need to begin the healing process.

> "Deliver my soul, O Lord, from lying lips, and from a deceitful tongue."
>
> (Psalm 120:2 NKJV)

Prayer: Dear Lord, I desire to be more honest before you. I know that as I admit the truth to you, you will deal with me, and the truth will make me free.

Lesson Application

Date: _____

Today I will:

_____

_____

_____

_____

_____

_____

_____

Progress Made/Prayer Answered:

Date: _____

_____

_____

_____

_____

_____

_____

"Do you like that?"

Often while observing something potentially objectionable on television—such as a scantily clad woman or a guy with his shirt off, my daughter would say, "Mommy do you like that?" or, "Is that yucky?"

She knew that there were things on television to which I objected. She would look to me for my approval when she saw something about which she was uncertain. She figured it was something I probably didn't want her to watch, and she was also learning what was appropriate for her and what wasn't.

She was allowing me to shape her thoughts and establish her boundaries. How wonderful! Then I wondered if I am the same way. How often do I ask my heavenly Father, "God, do you like that for me?

Is that cool or is that yucky?" It may look like a great business opportunity, but is it what God wants for me? I may think my attitude is fine, but it may actually be inappropriate. God sees things differently than us. What may seem perfectly OK with us may be totally inappropriate in God's eyes.

It's important for us to remain as a child before God and allow Him to shape and mold our way of thinking until we begin to think as He thinks and grow to know what His will is for us. It's wonderful when our children yearn to do what is pleasing in our eyes. Likewise, God loves it when we yearn to do what is pleasing in His.

> *"And whatsoever we ask, we receive of him, because we keep his commandments, and do those things that are pleasing in his sight."*
>
> (1 John 3:22 KJV)

Prayer: Dear Lord, I yearn to do what is pleasing in your eyes. Purify my heart. Help me to be more like you.

Lesson Application

Date: _____

Today I will:

_____

_____

_____

_____

_____

_____

_____

Progress Made/Prayer Answered:

Date: _____

_____

_____

_____

_____

_____

_____

"My best mommy is here today."

While busy around the house I happened to "tune in" long enough to notice the latest song by my five-year-old songwriter, vocalist. The song's chorus was, "My Best Mommy is Here Today," and I immediately wondered whether or not the song was prophetic.

Is her best mommy really here today? I asked myself. *Or is she buried under worry, stress or other obligations?*

Our children desire and need for us to be totally present and focused on the task at hand—rearing and nurturing them. Time goes by so quickly and we don't get another chance once they're grown.

At the same time, God expects us to be focused on the task at hand—our purpose for being here on this earth. What gifts, talents and skills has God put in us that He wants us to live out? Are you a shining example of the love of Christ? Is God's best Christian here today?

> *"Let your light so shine before men, that they may see your good works, and glorify your Father which is in heaven."*
>
> (Matthew 5:16 KJV)

Prayer: Lord, help me to walk in your grace so that I can do your will each day. I desire to be the best Christian I can be so that others will be drawn to you.

Lesson Application

Date: _____

Today I will:

_____

_____

_____

_____

_____

_____

_____

Progress Made/Prayer Answered:

Date: _____

_____

_____

_____

_____

_____

_____

"I'm getting bigger."

As was her daily routine, my daughter strolled into the bathroom to brush her teeth. But wait, something was different this time. As she stood at the bathroom counter she could see clear into the mirror on the wall—without her step stool.

"I'm bigger now, Mommy!" she exclaimed.

It was an exciting day for her. She realized that she was growing up—becoming a "big girl."

As Christians it is so easy to focus on what we've done wrong or how we've messed up. But it is important for us to take time out to acknowledge our success and growth.

Are there instances where in the past you would have spoken out in anger but today you held your peace? Rejoice!

Did you forgive and let go of a wrong done to you recently? If so, acknowledge the fact that you are growing as a Christian, and this will encourage you and motivate you onward. Take note of your areas of growth and rejoice at what God has done!

> *"Being confident of this, that he who began a good work in you will carry it on to completion until the day of Christ Jesus."*
>
> (Philippians 1:6 NIV)

Prayer: Dear Lord, please forgive me for not taking time to recognize the work you have done in my life—specifically in my character. I know you are not finished with me yet, but I rejoice in what you have already done. Thank you.

Lesson Application

Date: _____

Today I will:

_____

_____

_____

_____

_____

_____

_____

Progress Made/Prayer Answered:

Date: _____

_____

_____

_____

_____

_____

_____

"I want to pray for my friends."

My daughter and I were decorating for her 4th birthday party—a Princess Party—with every pink, glittery, princess accessory imaginable. It was to be a party fit for twelve little darling princesses. She was very excited.

"This is going to be so great!" she kept saying.

Then out of the blue she says, "Mommy, I want to pray for my friends."

"Okay," I said, but I didn't really see where that comment came from. But as I gave it more thought, I realized that out of her heart of gratitude was birthed a desire to pray for her friends. Her little heart was so overwhelmed with joy that it began to spill over and out, and manifested in her desire to pray for others.

God's lovingkindness towards us will cause us to do that—become *others* focused. When we take the time to recognize all the ways in which God blesses us—although we do not deserve it— it should cause our hearts to fill with joy. And when we take the time to enter into His presence, our joy becomes full.

Once our joy is full it's like a cup that runs over and onto other people in the form of prayer, encouragement and good deeds. When you come across something really good you just can't keep it to yourself. You've got to go tell somebody.

"You will show me the path of life; In your presence is fullness of joy; At your right hand are pleasures forevermore."

(Psalm 16:11 NKJV)

Prayer: Dear Lord, help me to develop an attitude of gratitude. Help me to become so full of joy in you that it spills over into my desire to pray for, encourage and do good for others.

Lesson Application

Date: _____

Today I will:

_____

_____

_____

_____

_____

_____

_____

Progress Made/Prayer Answered:

Date: _____

_____

_____

_____

_____

_____

_____

"Me first!"

We were on a play date with a family who had two other toddlers. The kids pulled out their little race cars and began racing around the first floor of the house. Although they seemed to be having a good time, I couldn't help but notice that the words "me first" became the resounding chorus among these four children.

"Me first!" one would say.

"No, me first!" the other would reply.

"Me first!" cried the third.

Not long after I'd hear, "Me first!" from the fourth.

Maybe these children were saying "me first" because their vocabulary was limited, but honestly, these children were saying "me first" because it's natural to say. It's normal at their developmental stage to be self-centered and self-absorbed.

However, there comes a point where we must grow up and out of the "me first" stage and learn to put God first. As mature Christians, we should desire to get to the place where, like the apostle Paul describes, he's not living to himself, but it is Christ who is living through him.

> *"I have been crucified with Christ and I no longer live, but Christ lives in me. The life I live in the body, I live by faith in the Son of God, who loved me and gave himself for me."*
>
> (Galatians 2:20 NIV)

Prayer: Dear Lord, I desire for you to reign on the throne of my heart. Please guide my heart and direct my paths. I long to be more like you.

Lesson Application

Date: _____

Today I will:

_____

_____

_____

_____

_____

_____

Progress Made/Prayer Answered:

Date: _____

_____

_____

_____

_____

_____

_____

"Jesus wants some milk!"

It was dinnertime.

"Honey, you have to drink your water before you can have some milk. You've not had enough water today," I explained to my daughter. She wasn't very happy. She continued to eat—solemnly—then a moment later she looked up and said,

"Jesus wants some milk."

"Oh, Jesus wants some milk?" I asked.

"Yes, me and Jesus."

I couldn't help but chuckle. At that point I realized that although only three years old, she recognized the authority of Jesus. She figured that if Jesus was requesting it, it would get done. And by association, if Jesus was her pal and He got milk, she would get some too. Her line of reasoning was correct.

God wants to shower us with blessings. All we have to do is position ourselves. Jesus encourages us to become one with Him by spending time in His Word and in prayer, praise and worship—just as Jesus is one with His Father. As a result, we can operate in more authority and life, in its fullest, will open up to us in ways we've never known before.

"If you remain in me and my words remain in you, ask whatever you wish, and it will be given you."
(John 15:7 NIV)

Prayer: Holy Spirit, help me to worship Christ in spirit and in truth. I thank you that I am becoming one with Christ and that I have authority in His name.

Lesson Application

Date: _____

Today I will:

_____

_____

_____

_____

_____

_____

_____

Progress Made/Prayer Answered:

Date: _____

_____

_____

_____

_____

_____

_____

"But Mommy, you're supposed to..."

Mommy..."

"Hmm?" I responded.

"Mommy, you're supposed to say, "yes."

"Okay...Yes, honey?" I replied back. *It served the same purpose. Wasn't "hmm" good enough?* But I'd established a pattern. My daughter would say or do certain things and I would say or do certain things in response.

But after a while, my daughter expected me to *always* say or do the same thing—which left me no room for flexibility or room to change my mind. She had put me in a box. I realized we often do this with God.

Since God did it this way before, He'll do it this way again.

When we get in a bind, we say, "God, you're supposed to…" But, if we don't like being put in a box how much more does God dislike it? Besides, God has way too many "tricks up His sleeve," so to speak, to be limited to one or two responses. Let God out of the box. God will respond, but how He responds is totally up to Him.

> *"And they shall know that I am the LORD their God, that brought them forth out of the land of Egypt, that I may dwell among them: I am the LORD their God."*
>
> (Exodus 29:46 KJV)

Prayer: Dear Lord, please forgive me for expecting you to do things a certain way. I recognize that you are an infinite God and you can respond to my situation in an infinite number of ways. Have your way in my life.

Lesson Application

Date: _____

Today I will:

_____

_____

_____

_____

_____

_____

_____

Progress Made/Prayer Answered:

Date: _____

_____

_____

_____

_____

_____

_____

"I'm busy."

"Honey, will you get my water bottle for me?"

"I'm busy," my three-year-old daughter replied.

"You're busy?" I inquired.

"I'm watching TV."

Okay. I was pretty stumped. Here is my three-year-old daughter who is too busy to bring me my water bottle—a really simple request—which is not too much to ask considering all the sacrifices I make for her each day. I took a deep breath.

Then I heard that still, small voice remind me of how I'm often too busy to do what He requests— "Will you pray with me for an hour? Will you visit your neighbor who is lonely and talk with her? Will you go tell that person about me?"

I never respond with the words, "No, I'm busy, Lord—" I guess I'm not as honest as my child. I just don't get around to doing it. But in lieu of the ultimate sacrifice that Jesus Christ made for us, know that whenever God asks us to do something, He has empowered and equipped us to accomplish it. Let's not make ourselves too busy. Our sacrifices are small in light of the ultimate price He paid.

"So Abram departed, as the LORD had spoken unto him."

(Genesis 12:4 KJV)

Prayer: Dear Lord. Please forgive me for not always making myself available to you as I should. Today I commit to obey the requests you make of me.

Lesson Application

Date: _____

Today I will:

_____

_____

_____

_____

_____

_____

_____

Progress Made/Prayer Answered:

Date: _____

_____

_____

_____

_____

_____

_____

"I don't like dinner anymore."

"Honey, you have to eat your dinner before you can have dessert," I said to my three year old.

"But I don't want dinner!" she replied.

"I know, but dinner is healthy for you."

"I don't like dinner anymore," she said affirmatively—hence resolving that if that's the way it has to be, she just won't do dinner anymore. She'll eliminate dinner from her repertoire and just do breakfast, lunch and dessert.

The problem is, there is no dessert if she doesn't eat dinner. Thus, she'll never get what she ultimately wants—the *prize* of dessert. Likewise, often we have to grit our teeth and bear the difficulties of life in order to get what we ultimately want. We cannot opt out of prayer, praise, study of the Word, fellowship with other believers—nor test and trials for that matter—and expect the abundant Christian life. We'll never have it. We must have a well-balanced life in order to have the sweet life in Christ.

> *"Consider it pure joy, my brothers, whenever you face trials of many kinds, because you know that the testing of your faith develops perseverance. Perseverance must finish its work so that you may be mature and complete, not lacking anything."*
>
> (James 1:2-4 NIV)

Prayer: Dear Lord, help me to endure the difficult times knowing that sweet taste of victory already belongs to me.

Lesson Application

Date: _____

Today I will:

_____

_____

_____

_____

_____

_____

_____

Progress Made/Prayer Answered:

Date: _____

_____

_____

_____

_____

_____

_____

"I want to go to this piggy bank again."

Every time I go through the drive-thru at a particular bank, the nice teller packs three delicious red suckers into an envelope for my children. One day after leaving the bank and enjoying his delightful sucker, my three-year-old son said, "Mommy, I want to go to this piggy bank again!"

After getting over the fact that he called a federally insured savings and loan institution a piggy bank, I realized that he had come to a reasonable conclusion.

When mommy goes to this piggy bank, I get a sucker. Hence, I want to go here again.

Often we long for our Christian walk to be as simple and to achieve such swift results.

When I pray, I receive my answer instantaneously. When I fast, what I'm believing God for arrives *immediately. Hence, I want to pray and fast again and again!*Well, sometimes that happens. But often when we pray, God's answer is to wait, and when we ask God for something it usually takes time to materialize.

However, we cannot cease doing the right thing. You may not get what you're seeking right away, but keep praying, keep believing and keep asking. God is always faithful to hear, answer and deliver.

> *"Keep on asking and it will be given you; keep on seeking and you will find; keep on knocking [reverently] and [the door] will be opened to you."*
> (Matthew 7:7 AMP)

Prayer: Dear Lord, help me to be more patient and diligent. With your help, I will pray until I hear, seek until I find and believe until I receive.

Lesson Application

Date: _____

Today I will:

_____

_____

_____

_____

_____

_____

Progress Made/Prayer Answered:

Date: _____

_____

_____

_____

_____

_____

_____

"I want you to help me, Daddy!"

I want you to help me, Daddy!" my daughter says while tying her shoe.

Now my daughter had already mastered the skill of shoe-tying but she just loved enlisting her daddy's help for just about anything. I reasoned that she enjoyed his company and she took pride in his abilities. Whenever he completed the task, her eyes lit up and she gave him the biggest smile. Oh, how a little girl knows how to make her daddy feel special!

We should be the same way with our heavenly Father. We should eagerly desire God's help—not just when it's an emergency, but every day and in every situation, because God's way and God's help in our lives produces the very best results.

"In all your ways know, recognize, and acknowledge Him, and He will direct and make straight and plain your paths."

(Proverbs 3:6 AMP)

Prayer: Heavenly Father, I desire your help in every area of my life. I know that your involvement in the details of my life will yield the very best results.

Lesson Application

Date: _____

Today I will:

_____

_____

_____

_____

_____

_____

_____

Progress Made/Prayer Answered:

Date: _____

_____

_____

_____

_____

_____

_____

"I want to go bye-bye."

The day was dark, cloudy, snowy and cold—a typical winter day in our town. After being stuck in the house during a string of such lack-luster days, my daughter comes up to me, sighs and says, "Mommy, I want to go bye-bye."

No further explanation needed. She was tired of being at home. She longed to go some place and experience something different. Are you at that place today? Are you tired of being in the same spot? Do you long to graduate on to something different or more exciting? Spiritually, are you in a place that you are no longer proud to call home? We all go through this phase.

When we as adults find ourselves bored, stuck or just plain tired of being in the same situation day in and day out, often it's a sign. It's a sign that we're not doing something God has destined for us to do.

It may be only one thing, but we must make time to involve ourselves in that one thing—whether it's praying more, spending time in His Word, or taking steps to fulfill the unique call of God on our lives. When we spend time with God, our joy increases and our inner passion is ignited. As I tell my children, boredom is a choice. When we are fully engaged in every aspect of life as God has designed, we'll find we're always graduating to life's next adventure of faith, and we never have time to be bored.

> *"But you— keep your eye on what you're doing; accept the hard times along with the good; keep the Message alive; do a thorough job as God's servant."*
> (2 Timothy 4:5 The Message)

Prayer: Dear Lord, I know sometimes I feel stuck, tired and just plain bored with my life. Please help me to discover joy and fulfillment in the life you have for me.

Lesson Application

Date: _____

Today I will:

_____

_____

_____

_____

_____

_____

_____

Progress Made/Prayer Answered:

Date: _____

_____

_____

_____

_____

_____

_____

About the Author

Anita S. Lane, affectionately dubbed "The Mommy Lady," is career woman turned stay-at-home mom of four young children. She is the founder and editor of *Keeping Family First* online magazine.

A prolific writer, Anita is committed to pursuing her passion for encouraging other moms. "My heart goes out to every mom in America. We lead very busy, complex lives today. We need to encourage one another and *every* mom needs to know that she is not alone."

In January of 2005, Anita launched *Keeping Family First* online magazine (www.KeepingFamilyFirst. org). *Keeping Family First* "expert" moms and dads write on topics ranging from fitness, health, parenting, business, fashion, finance and more. The magazine offers hundreds of resources and features new authors and exclusive celebrity interviews. In September of 2005, *Keeping Family First* for dads, (www.KFFDads.org) was launched.

Prior to becoming a stay-at-home mom, Anita earned her bachelor's degree in political science and a master's degree in public policy from the University of Michigan. She worked for over ten years in the field of community development—managing and marketing programs, and procuring millions of dollars for family and youth-serving organizations in the city of Detroit.

A devoted Christian, Anita was licensed to the ministry at the young age of 25. Today, her primary ministry is to the family—hers and others', as well. In a warm, down-to-earth and often humorous fashion, Anita writes on the topic of motherhood as well as societal and policy issues that affect today's families.

Anita authors a column for moms at www.JustForMom.com. She writes a regular column for Hope for Women magazine and is a contributing author in the August 2006 release, *Chicken Soup for the African American Woman's Soul.*

Anita is an author, freelance writer and columnist. She enjoys traveling and entertaining friends. She resides in Grosse Pointe, Michigan with her husband and four young children.

Pleasant
Word

To order additional copies of this title call:
1-877-421-READ (7323)
or please visit our web site at
www.pleasantwordbooks.com

If you enjoyed this quality custom published book,
drop by our web site for more books and information.

www.winepressgroup.com
"Your partner in custom publishing."

9 781414 109275